AS THE DEER

The Christian Salvation Experience

PAMELA L. DELPH

Trilogy Christian Publishers
A Wholly Owned Subsidary of Trinity Broadcasting Network
2442 Michelle Drive
Tustin, CA 92780

For information, address Trilogy Christian Publishing
Rights Department, 2442 Michelle Drive, Tustin, Ca 92780.
Trilogy Christian Publishing/ TBN and colophon are trademarks of Trinity Broadcasting Network.

For information about special discounts for bulk purchases, please contact Trilogy Christian Publishing.

Manufactured in the United States of America

10 9 8 7 6 5 4 3 2 1

Library of Congress Cataloging-in-Publication Data is available.

ISBN 978-1-64088-973-6 (Print Book)
ISBN 978-1-64088- 974-3 (ebook)

It is with much thanksgiving and a heart filled with gratitude that I dedicate this book to my heavenly Father, my Lord and Savior Christ Jesus, and the precious Holy Spirit of God. Without the love of the Father, the redeeming work of Christ, and the Holy Spirit's wisdom, teaching and bringing things to my remembrance, this book would not have been possible. I am eternally grateful for all that God has done, is doing, and will continue to do in and through my life. To him be *all* the glory! Amen

Contents

Introduction

This book was originally designed to be a follow-up for those who have recently received Christ as their Lord and Savior (a new Christian who just had become born again or born anew).

Many times, when I was leading someone to the Lord through preaching/teaching the Gospel and directing them through a prayer of salvation, I often found that I did not have any further access to them, never seeing them again. Hence, there is no continued ability of further input to disciple them (herein is trust in God and my prayers that he would be able to disciple them as he sees fit and connect them to the right fellowship). On these such occasions of evangelism, I wanted to have ready materials to hand them, which could point them in the right direction of discipleship in the interim for those not yet connected to a Christian assembly, church, or Christian mentor.

While writing this book, the feedback from others (family and friends) brought awareness of other possible uses for this book. Things that were discussed were the use for salvation(s) and the understanding of evangelism to those who are oversees or in other states and countries as well as a discipleship tool. Also discussed were uses for teaching and training in evangelism, classes for new members and new converts, and Bible studies on basic disciplines and studies on our Christian benefits (see sections 2 and 3 of this book).

And so much more as this can be a handy tool for kingdom purposes.

It is my sincere prayer that many will come to know and understand the fullness of Christ Jesus as Lord and Savior, and become productive citizens in the kingdom of God both now and throughout eternity through the teachings and training of this book. May the Lord lead you and guide you in all that you do in him. May his grace be with you always.

> And the peace of God, which passeth all understanding keep you hearts and your minds through Christ Jesus. (Philippians 4:7)

> Pamela L. Delph, President and Founder World Outreach Ministries International, Inc.

> For this cause I bow my knees unto the Father of our Lord Jesus Christ, Of whom the whole family in heaven and earth is named, That he would grant you, according to the riches of his glory, to be strengthened with might by his Spirit in the inner man; That Christ may dwell in your hearts by faith; that ye, being rooted and grounded in love, May be able to comprehend with all saints what is the breadth, and length, and depth, and height; And to know the love of Christ, which passeth knowledge, that ye might be filled with all the fulness of God. (Ephesians. 3:14–9)

SECTION 1

Salvation Experience

And as Moses lifted up the serpent in the wilderness, even
so must the Son of man be lifted up: That whosoever
believeth in him should not perish, but have eternal life.
—John 3:14–15

For God so loved the world, that he gave his only
begotten Son, that whosoever believeth in him
should not perish, but have everlasting life.
—John 3:16

For God sent not his Son into the world to condemn the
world; but that the world through him might be saved.
—John 3:17

If you confess with your mouth the Lord Jesus
and believe in your heart that God has raise him
from the dead, you shall be saved. For with the
heart man believeth unto righteousness; and with
the mouth confession is made unto salvation.
—Romans 10:8–10

What must we do to be saved?

The Gospel of our God is the Good News of how man can be restored to right relationship with God, having their sins forgiven and live in the way that God originally designed for us. The Gospel encompasses hearing the Gospel, believing, repenting, confessing of faith—believing in the death, burial, and resurrection of our Lord Jesus Christ as payment for our sins.

Hear the Gospel of Salvation in God

Man cannot save himself. God made a way of salvation.

> To whom shall we go, you have the words of eternal life. And we believe and are sure that you are the Christ, Son of the Living God. (John 6:38)

(See also other biblical references to eternal life: Matthew 19:16, Luke 10:25, John 17:2–3, Acts 13:48.)

Man's dilemma: Sin—eternal separation from fellowship and right standing with God.

Sin is wrongdoing, whether it is by things you've done wrong, left undone, or thought wrong that are contrary to or a breaking of God's laws, commandments, and/or holy standards.

Sin results in:

1) right relationship with God being broken (eternal separation/death if not rectified),

2) penalty/judgment for the offense(s) (God is just; therefore, he must punish sin. See: Exodus 34:7, Jeremiah 30:11).

Sin is being guilty of error/wrongdoing as defined by God. Without payment of sin, there will only be judgment, condemnation, eternal separation from God, and yes, hell for all eternity.

> For I determined not to know any thing among you, save Jesus Christ and Him crucified. (1 Corinthians 2:2)

The Apostle Paul was adamant about one thing, "Jesus Christ and him crucified." Why? Because without the crucifixion of Christ, there would be no payment great enough to pay for our sins. We would still be guilty today, only to be judged guilty at the Great White Throne Judgment of God and sent to hell with the devil and the fallen demonic angels.

Hell was originally made for Lucifer (Satan, the devil) and his fallen/unclean angels (demons) (Isaiah 14:9–17). Unfortunately, humans who refuse to accept Jesus' atoning work and rebel against God will ultimately end up in hell too, if they don't repent.

But thank God for his ultimate sacrifice and love for us that he did not leave us that way, but gave us a way to be redeemed. God the Father made a way of payment for our sins by Jesus Christ's sacrifice on the cross of Calvary.

Believe

Believing is not just head knowledge. Head knowledge is just that, something your mind knows, whether true, or fictional, or knowledge of a fact (like knowing that George Washington was the first president of the United States).

Head knowledge of God's existence is not enough. The devil and demons believe and know of the existence of God, but that's not going to save them.

> Thou believest that there is one God;
> thou doest well: the devils also believe,
> and tremble. (James 2:19)

So what is believing? Biblical believing here is not only knowing God exists, but also transferring your trust from your own self-efforts (which will never be enough) to trusting in God to save you.

Example: You see a chair. You know the chair can hold you up if you sit in it. But the chair cannot hold you up until you get up physically from where you are at and physically "sit" in it. It's the same way with believing God to forgive and save you. You must transfer your trust from your own self-righteousness and self-efforts, and receive Jesus's payment and finished work on the cross for you.

And they said, Believe on the Lord Jesus Christ, and thou shalt be saved, and thy house. (Acts 16:31)

And he [Jesus] said unto them, Go ye into all the world, and preach the gospel to every creature. He that believeth and is baptized shall be saved; but he that believeth not shall be damned. (Mark 16:15–16)

Repent Your Sins

> Then Peter said unto them, Repent, and
> be baptized every one of you in the name
> of Jesus Christ for the remission of sins,
> and ye shall receive the gift of the Holy
> Ghost. (Acts 2:38)

Repentance is not just sorrow and guilty feelings of regret or wrongdoing and thinking (sin). Repentance also means that you *turn away* from such wrong activities and/or thoughts. (Examples: If you are committing adultery, you stop such activities effective immediately! If you're a liar, you stop lying. If you're a thief, you stop stealing and so on.)

> Talk no more so exceeding proudly; let not
> arrogancy come out of your mouth: for
> the LORD is a God of knowledge, and by
> him Actions are weighed. (1 Samuel 2:3)

Confess

Confession is admitting that you cannot save yourself and have a need for God to forgive you of your past, present, and future sins, and accepting him as Lord and Savior of your life.

Confession must be acknowledged out loud because confession is not only a heart attitude, but also a public declaration of your acceptance of God's way of salvation by Christ Jesus.

> Whosoever therefore shall confess me before men, him will I confess also before my Father which is in heaven. But whosoever shall deny me before men, him will I also deny before my Father which is in heaven. (Matthew 10:32–33)

Ask Jesus to come into your heart and be your Lord and Savior now and forever, out loud through prayer.

Prayer of Salvation

Important: To be prayed *out loud* and sincerely.

Heavenly Father, I come to you in the Name of Jesus, through his precious blood. I ask you to forgive me of all my sins—past, present, and future—from things I have done wrong, thought wrong, and left undone. I repent and choose to turn away from all wrong behavior and thoughts. (List any and all things that come to mind and ask God to bring to remembrance any other sins you need to repent of.)

I choose to forgive and release all person(s) and/or groups of people from all unforgiveness, wrongs, and resentments, whether perceived or actual, and whether they deserve it or not, because I want you to forgive me of all my sins and faults.

Jesus, I ask you to come into my heart and be my Lord and Savior now and throughout all eternity. Teach me your ways. Guide and lead me all the rest

my days. I thank you for forgiving me
and loving me.
  In Jesus's name. Amen

 Now that you have prayed out loud the salvation prayer, believe in your heart that you *are* saved (a.k.a. born again). No one can ever take that away from you!

The Difference between Facts, Faith, and Feelings

Please understand the difference between facts, faith, and feelings, and being strong in your new life in Christ.

Facts

Definition: a thing that is indisputably the case. More generally, fact is something that is proven to be true. It's important to distinguish between *fact* and fiction. A thing that *can* be shown to be *true*, to exist, or to *have* happened. Something that actually exists.

Biblical facts. What God says about you, your salvation, his kingdom, his principles, and his laws as stated in the scriptures are all facts. These facts of God are eternal in nature and never change.

> Heaven and earth shall pass away: but my words shall not pass away. (Mark 13:31)

> Jesus Christ the same yesterday, and to day, and for ever. (Hebrews 13:8)

Faith

Definition: (noun)
1. complete trust or confidence in someone or something;
2. strong belief in God or in the doctrines of a religion, based on spiritual apprehension rather than proof.

Faith simply means believing that something is true, and then committing our lives to it.

In the Bible, "faith" means believing in God and in what Christ has done for us to make our salvation possible, and then committing ourselves to him. In other words, faith has two parts to it, and both are equally important.

The first part is *belief*—belief that God exists and that he loves us and sent his Son into the world to save us. Faith isn't a vague hope that God might exist; it is a definite belief that what the Bible says about him is true. The Bible says:

> Without faith it is impossible to please God, because anyone who comes to him must believe that he exists and that he rewards those who earnestly seek him. (Hebrews11:6)

The second part of faith is *commitment*—a definite decision not only to believe in our minds that Christ can save us, but to put our lives into his hands and trust him alone for our salvation. True faith not only believes Christ can save us, but actually trusts him to do it. The Bible says:

> For it is by grace you have been saved, through faith. Not of works, lest any man should boast. (Ephesians 2:8–9)

Feelings (Emotions)

Definition:
1. an emotional state or reaction,
2. feelings are temporary and change as circumstances change.

Feelings are based on external events or situations and are temporary. Feelings are temporary and influenced by circumstances.

To base decisions and faith upon something that changes like the wind is foolish. That is why your faith/salvation should be based upon the unchanging Word of God (facts as written in scripture) and God's promises versus upon feelings that can change at any given moment.

Just because you don't "feel" saved or don't "feel" like a Christian does not mean that you are suddenly not a Christian. You made a decision that is eternally based upon the fact of the Gospel that you heard and/or read, believed, and accepted. God backs up his promises, and they are for all eternity. He doesn't change his mind or take it back. So rest assured that despite your feelings, you are saved.

> In whom ye also trusted, after that ye heard the word of truth, the gospel of your salvation: in whom also after that ye believed, ye were sealed with that holy Spirit of promise, Which is the earnest of our inheritance until the redemption of the purchased possession, unto the praise of his glory. (Ephesians 1:12–14)

Blessed be the God and Father of our Lord Jesus Christ, which according to his abundant mercy hath begotten us again unto a lively hope by the resurrection of Jesus Christ from the dead, To an inheritance incorruptible, and undefiled, and that fadeth not away, reserved in heaven for you, Who are kept by the power of God through faith unto salvation ready to be revealed in the last time. (1 Peter 1:3–5)

SECTION 2

New Life in Christ

Therefore if any man be in Christ, he is a new creature: old things are passed away; behold, all things are become new.
—2 Corinthians 5:17

And be not conformed to this world: but be ye transformed by the renewing of your mind, that ye may prove what is that good, and acceptable, and perfect, will of God.
—Romans 12:2

Word

Word of God or Holy Scriptures

I cannot emphasize enough the importance of getting to know the Word of God (a.k.a. the Holy Scriptures). Not only will knowing the Word of God strengthen your faith, but it will also protect you from counterfeit religions, teachings, and philosophies.

> Till we all come in the unity of the faith, and of the knowledge of the Son of God, unto a perfect (mature) man, unto the measure of the stature of the fulness of Christ: That we henceforth be no more children, tossed to and fro, and carried about with every wind of doctrine, by the sleight of men, and cunning craftiness, whereby they lie in wait to deceive. (Ephesians 4:13–14)

Until now, you have been educated by and learned worldly ways, many of which are corrupt, or have been tainted with sin, doubt, unbelief, pride of life, lust of the eyes, and so on.

It is important, now that you are a Christian and a new citizen of the heavenly Kingdom, that you educate yourself with God's ways and God's kingdom principles by renewing your mind with the Holy Scriptures and sound kingdom teaching. This takes time, but with consistent effort, eventually, your daily efforts will all add up to mature you in your knowledge of your salvation and all its benefits.

When you purchase a new car or cell phone that you don't know all the features of or how to use it properly or even to the fullest potential, the manufacturer provides you with a manual. The Bible is our manual given to us by our manufacturer, God, written through his chosen messengers who were inspired by the Holy Spirit of God.

May I suggest that you pray before you read the Word of God and ask our heavenly Father to help you understand what you are reading.

> All scripture is given by inspiration of God, and is profitable for doctrine, for reproof, for correction, for instruction in righteousness: That the man of God may be perfect, thoroughly furnished unto all good works. (2 Timothy 3:16–17)

> Thy word have I hid in mine heart, that I might not sin against thee. (Psalm 119:11)

Studying the Word of God

Reading the Word of God is great and needed to familiarize yourself with its contents and principles, but eventually, you will want to *study* the Word of God. The adventure of studying, learning, examining, and exploring the Bible in depth has many benefits (some of which we will cover latter in this book.)

Many people rely on preachers, pastors, apostles, bishops, etc. to teach us the Word. But how do you know that they are accurate or not teaching you something erroneous? There is no substitute for studying and knowing the Word for yourself. The Berean Christians were commended by God for studying the Word to see that those things that they had heard were true. They did not just take it point blank from the messengers; instead, they chose to confirm the validity of those things which they heard by studying the scriptures.

> And the brethren immediately sent away Paul and Silas by night unto Berea: who coming thither went into the synagogue of the Jews. These were more noble than those in Thessalonica, in that they received the word with all readiness of mind, and searched the scriptures daily, whether those things were so. (Acts 17:10–11)

> Study to shew thyself approved unto God, a workman that needeth not to be ashamed, rightly dividing the word of truth. (2 Timothy 2:15)

Memorizing (let the Word dwell within you richly!)

> Let the word of Christ dwell in you richly in all wisdom; teaching and admonishing one another in psalms and hymns and

spiritual songs, singing with grace in your
hearts to the Lord. (Colossians 3:16)

But the Comforter, which is the Holy
Ghost, whom the Father will send in my
name, he shall teach you all things, and
bring all things to your remembrance,
whatsoever I have said unto you. (John
14:26)

The Word of God will keep you in times of challenge,
but if you don't first put it *in*, there will be nothing to fall back
on. It is the work of the Holy Spirit of God that will bring to
your remembrance those things that you have learned, studied, and/or memorized as you need them.

Thy word have I hid in mine heart, that
I might not sin against thee. (Psalm
119:11)

The Word of God brings correction and direction,
keeping you in the truth of the Word. In times of temptation, the Word of God will be your stay.

There hath no temptation taken you but
such as is common to man: but God is
faithful, who will not suffer you to be
tempted above that ye are able; but will
with the temptation also make a way to
escape, that ye may be able to bear it. (1
Corinthians 10:13)

Thy word is a lamp unto my feet, and a light unto my path. (Psalm 119:105)

All scripture is given by inspiration of God, and is profitable for doctrine, for reproof, for correction, for instruction in righteousness: That the man of God may be perfect, thoroughly furnished unto all good works. (2 Timothy 3:16–17)

Praise

Praise is different from worship. Praise is declaring the attributes of God and exalting him for his goodness. Praise may speak about who God is without necessarily talking to him directly (i.e. like in a song about God, or what he has done, or how we feel about God).

Praise can be used as a weapon to renew your confidence in who or how mighty God is and can bring confusion to the enemy's camp.

> But thou are holy, O thou that inhabitest
> the praises of Israel. (Psalm 22:3)

Example of a praise song by Michael W. Smith

> Great is the Lord, he is holy and just
> By his power, we trust in his love
> Great is the Lord, he is faithful and true
> By his mercy, he proves he is love
>
> Great is the Lord and worthy of glory
> Great is the Lord and worthy of praise
> Great is the Lord
> Now lift up your voice
> Now lift up your voice
> Great is the Lord
> Great is the Lord

Worship

Worship on the other hand is inscribing honor directly to God himself, ascribing "worth-ship" to him directly!

Many church services or assemblies may begin with praise songs and eventually move into a worship mode. Worship is no longer about me, but about and to him and directed to him only!

As some local assemblies move into a mode of worship, they come into one accord. Then at a certain point in the worship, you may experience the "high" or *tehillah*" worship of God. This free-flowing form of worship is spontaneous and comes from deep within the believer's heart of reverence, gratitude, love, and true, heartfelt worship. There is nothing that sounds more beautiful than a group of believers all worshipping the Lord from their hearts with everything that is within them in adoration, expressing reverence in worship to the one and only wise God.

Worship is not only for corporate settings, but also can and should be in your individual times of fellowship with God too.

Prayer

Prayer is one of the most basic forms of communication with God and should be addressed with respect as to who God is as your Creator and who holds your life in his hand.

As a child of God, we approach God from a position of faith-believing, with respect and confidence that he will hear us and answer according to his will. Religiousness is not necessary. It will *not* add any credibility to your prayers to use King James's style language or add many repetitive phrases, or try to impress him with your grammar. Just be yourself and communicate your prayers to God with thanksgiving, sincerity, in humbleness, and in a pure childlike faith.

> And fear not them which kill the body but are not able to kill the soul: but rather fear him (God) which is able to destroy both soul and body in hell. (Matthew 10:28)

> If any of you lack wisdom, let him ask of God, that giveth to all men liberally, and upbraideth not; and it shall be given him. But let him ask in faith, nothing wavering. For he that wavereth is like a wave of the sea driven with the wind and tossed. For let not that man think that

he shall receive any thing of the Lord. (James 1:5–7)

Seeing then that we have a great high priest, that is passed into the heavens, Jesus the Son of God, let us hold fast our profession. For we have not an high priest which cannot be touched with the feeling of our infirmities; but was in all points tempted like as we are, yet without sin. Let us therefore come boldly unto the throne of grace, that we may obtain mercy, and find grace to help in time of need. (Hebrews 14:14–16)

Prayer should always be addressed to: the heavenly Father, in the Name of Jesus.

Jesus himself answering his disciple's request to teach them how to pray said:

After this manner therefore pray ye: Our Father which art in heaven, Hallowed be thy name. Thy kingdom come, Thy will be done in earth, as it is in heaven. Give us this day our daily bread. And forgive us our debts, as we forgive our debtors. And lead us not into temptation, but deliver us from evil: For thine is the kingdom, and the power, and the glory, for ever. Amen. (Matthew 6:9–15)

For if ye forgive men their trespasses, your heavenly Father will also forgive

you: But if ye forgive not men their trespasses, neither will your Father forgive
your trespasses. (Matthew 6:9–15)

Prayer can take on many forms. We will briefly discuss the following types of prayer: requests, supplication,
intercession.

Requests

> Be careful for nothing; but in every thing
> by prayer and supplication with thanks-
> giving let your requests be made known
> unto God. (Philippians 4:6)

God knows before you ask him what you need and is
waiting to release the answer(s) to your request. However,
he is not obligated to answer our request(s) the way we want
Him to. His answers may be: yes, no, wait, etc.

Don't try to put God in a box by trying to figure out
how he is going to do something. He is God and God alone.
God is extremely resourceful and rarely does anything the
same way twice. Yet if he so choses to repeat a thing, who
are we to say otherwise. Once I prayed for 'money' to buy a
specific item I needed desperately - but instead, much to my
surprise, I received the actual Item! Once you ask Him, leave
it up to Him to answer in the best way He sees fit.

Needs vs. wants.

> Ye ask, and receive not, because ye ask
> amiss, that ye may consume it upon your
> lusts. (James 4:3)

God knows what you truly need and what is a "covetous" request. He is not obligated to give you things that are frivolous, yet no request is too small or bothersome for him. The Lord also knows what you like and what you have need of. Trust him to give you what is right for you. This may not be what someone else has because what they have may not necessarily be right for you.

> Ask, and it shall be given you; seek, and ye shall find; knock, and it shall be opened unto you: For every one that asketh receiveth; and he that seeketh findeth; and to him that knocketh it shall be opened. (Matthew 7:7–8)

Supplications

Supplications, by definition, is ask(ing) for something earnestly or humbly: entreat, appeal, petition, etc.

Supplication is the form of which most of our prayers take when we come before God with our list of wants, needs, desires, or to ask on behalf of others the blessings we want to see done for them. Supplication can also be asking for help and/or grace in our time of need.

> Be careful for nothing; but in everything by prayer and supplication with thanksgiving let your requests be made known unto God. (Philippians 4:6)

> Yet ye have not, because ye ask not. Ye ask, and receive not, because ye ask amiss,

that ye may consume it upon your lusts. (James 4:2b–3)

Let us therefore come boldly unto the throne of grace, that we may obtain mercy, and find grace to help in time of need. (Hebrews 4:16)

Once we submit our request(s) to God in faith, we trust him to answer according to his perfect will, sovereignty, power, and timing.

Intercession

Definition: (noun)
1. the action of intervening on behalf of another;
    E.g. "Through the intercession of friends, I was able to obtain her a sinecure."
    Synonyms: mediation, intermediation, arbitration, conciliation, negotiation; intervention, involvement; pleading, petition, entreaty, agency; diplomacy.
    E.g. "The hostages were released after intercession by trained negotiators."
2. the action of saying a prayer on behalf of another person.
    E.g. "prayers of intercession"

And this is the confidence that we have in him, that, if we ask any thing according to his will, he heareth us: And if we know that he hear us, whatsoever we ask, we

> know that we have the petitions that we
> desired of him. (1 John 5:14–15)

Here, I will briefly discuss two basic forms of intercession: for salvation of others and for other urgent situations. (Please refer to my book on prayer for further studies of this topic matter.)

(Intersession) For salvation of others. One of the best ways to know God's will in prayer is to know what the Word of God says concerning a matter. For example: it is always right to pray for salvation for a person you know because the Word of God tells us that it is his desire for *all* men to be saved.

> For this is good and acceptable in the sight of God our Saviour; *Who will have all men to be saved,* and to come unto the knowledge of the truth. (1 Timothy 2:3–4; emphasis added)

Although God wants all men be saved and come unto the knowledge of the truth, not all will. Some will foolishly reject God, his ways, and sadly reject his gracious gift of salvation through the Messiah, Jesus the Christ.

As long as a person still has breath, there is still a chance for them to repent and ask God to save them. Even if it is on their deathbed. It matters not how "wicked" or "evil" they have been. If they call upon the name of Jesus in faith, repent, and pray for salvation, God will pardon, forgive, and save as he has said in his Word.

(Intercession) For other urgent situations. Example: Abraham and Lot (Abraham's intercession)

When Abraham found out the plans of God to wipe out Sodom and Gomorrah, he immediately and instinctively started interceding on behalf of the "righteous" that lived there (Genesis 18:17–32). The result—God remembered Abraham's prayer and sent his holy angels to rescue Lot and his immediate family before he released the judgment and destruction of that region.

> And it came to pass, when God destroyed the cities of the plain, that God remembered Abraham, and sent Lot out of the midst of the overthrow, when he overthrew the cities in the which Lot dwelt. (Genesis 19:29)

Sincere, heartfelt prayers are often effective when interceding for others:

> Confess your faults one to another, and pray one for another, that ye may be healed. The <u>effectual fervent</u> prayer of a righteous man availeth much. (James 5:16)

Fervent is defined as G1756, Strong's Concordance = "*energeo*" (en-ergy-eh'-o) or "to be active, efficient: effectual (fervent), be mighty in, shew forth."

Fervent is an adjective, which means, "having or displaying a passionate intensity."

It is not necessarily tears, emotions, or witty speech (pretense); but the sincere, heartfelt, ardent prayers of the believer, prayed in faith and belief that gets the attention and response of heaven. Often, what is needed is that sincere, childlike faith, and prayers prayed in true love of and from the heart.

Communion

Then Jesus said unto them, Verily, verily,
I say unto you, Except ye eat the flesh of
the Son of man, and drink his blood, ye
have no life in you. (John 6:53)

As in the above scripture, Jesus himself emphasized the importance of partaking in the communion (covenant) meal. His flesh, which was sacrificed for us, and his blood that was shed for us, purchased, paid for, and provides for us forgiveness of sins, the final atonement, payment for ours sins, and promise of eternal life in right standing with God.

To better understand communion, let's take a look at a biblical "covenant" first, of which some key aspects are but not limited to: *covenant meal, sacrifice, trade agreement of two or more parties, oath—to protect the other with your very life, and remembrance.*

The covenant was a traditional form of agreement in the culture of biblical times, much like our modern-day legal contracts or wills. Unlike our modern-day contracts, which can be broken randomly, a true covenant could only be broken at the death of one of the participants. A biblical covenant was sealed by the shedding of blood (a "sacrifice"), covenant meal, and a trade agreement of exchange of the time/talents and/or abilities of both parties with the agreement and promise to uphold the covenant with their very life! (Hence the phrase, "Till death do us part," which some cultures still use in a wedding ceremony. Marriage is one of the biblical covenants.)

Remembrance

The biblical sacrifice was often full of blood and gory, affecting the memory of the participants with potent sights and smells, something that was not soon forgotten. This is where we get the term, "remembrance" in Holy Communion. When we participate in Holy Communion, the scriptures from 1 Corinthians 11:23–29 are often recited, reminding us as to why we are partaking and what we are proclaiming in this covenant ceremony. Remembering Jesus's sacrifice on the cross of Calvary for us and what he had paid for in this gruesome sacrifice of himself that he willingly and lovingly did for us.

> For I have received of the Lord that which also I delivered unto you, that the Lord Jesus the same night in which he was betrayed took bread: And when he had given thanks, he brake it, and said, Take, eat: this is my body, which is broken for you: this do in remembrance of me. After the same manner also he took the cup, when he had supped, saying, this cup is the new testament in my blood: this do ye, as oft as ye drink it, in remembrance of me. For as often as ye eat this bread, and drink this cup, ye do shew the Lord's death till he come. Wherefore whosoever

shall eat this bread, and drink this cup of
the Lord, unworthily, shall be guilty of
the body and blood of the Lord. But let
a man examine himself, and so let him
eat of that bread, and drink of that cup.
For he that eateth and drinketh unworthily, eateth and drinketh damnation to
himself, not discerning the Lord's body.
(1 Corinthians 11:23–29)

With Christ

The cup of blessing which we bless, is
it not the communion of the blood of
Christ? The bread which we break, is
it not the communion of the body of
Christ? (1 Corinthians 10:16)

Eucharist

Eucharist, a religious term for communion elements
used in the ceremonial communion (covenant) meal, con-
sisting of the Bread and the Fruit of the Vine (grape juice or
wine).

The bread represents the *body* of our Lord and Savior,
which was sacrificed for us.

The wine or grape juice (fruit of the vine) represents the
blood of our Lord and Savior, which was shed for us. Both the
"body" and the "blood" should be served and received by all
during the communion ceremony.

Then Jesus said unto them, Verily, verily, I say unto you, Except ye eat the flesh

of the Son of man, and drink his blood,
ye have no life in you. Whoso eateth my
flesh, and drinketh my blood, hath eternal life; and I will raise him up at the last
day. (John 6:53–54)

His Presence

You can rest assured that as you either individually or
corporately gather to celebrate the communion meal, pray,
worship, or any other Christian function that Jesus himself
will be present and participate. He is very alive and very present. Whether you see him or not, he sees all, hears all, and
knows all. Often, you can feel his presence.

For where two or three are gathered
together in my name, there am I in the
midst of them. (Matthew 18:20)

Fellowship

Fellowship—definition: (noun)
1. friendly association, especially with people who share one's interests;

    E.g. "They valued fun and good fellowship as the cement of the community."

    Synonyms: companionship, companionability, sociability, comradeship, fraternization, camaraderie, friendship, mutual support, mutual respect, mutual liking; amiability, amity, affability, geniality, kindliness, cordiality, intimacy
2. social intercourse, social contact, association, closeness, togetherness, solidarity.

    E.g. "a community bound together in fellowship"

Good fellowship is necessary for the believers. Through fellowship, we create relationships with other believers who can watch over us, to keep us from drifting away from God's truth, good doctrine, and may even provide a safe place for us to receive encouragement, hope, prayer, and/or personal ministry. We also may be able to encourage others, praying for and ministering to them as well.

You may have heard the phrase, "No man is an island to himself." Could you see the danger in being isolated from other believers, also how the dangers of pride, self-righteousness, arrogance, and unteachable attitudes could creep in? Another danger of being isolated is feeling all alone (feelings of loneliness, depression, no hope, and abandonment) as well as the possibility of drifting away from sound doctrine, or creating a false doctrine(s) within yourself.

If you have been hurt before from a local assembly, other believers, or ministry leadership, may I strongly suggest you pray and ask God to heal you as you forgive them? Ask God to direct you to a safe assembly of believers (yes, this may mean that you have to travel further than originally desired but believe me, it will be well worth it.)

Fellowship with God

Fellowship with God himself is so very vital! Developing a relationship with him is necessary as a believer. After all, it is with him that we will answer to, and it is with him that we will spend eternity.

Jesus himself spoke of the difference between someone who "calls" themselves a Christian and does many religious acts versus someone who as a Christian develops a right relationship with God. Time spent with God, getting to know his heart on matters, what he expects from us, and doing his will, spending quality time developing a close relationship with him are key.

> Not every one that saith unto me, Lord, Lord, shall enter into the kingdom of heaven; but he that doeth the will of my Father which is in heaven. Many will say to me in that day, Lord, Lord, have we not prophesied in thy name? and in thy name have cast out devils? and in thy

name done many wonderful works? And then will I profess unto them, I never knew you: depart from me, ye that work iniquity. (Matthew 7:21–23)

With the body of Christ (the church universal)

Sometimes, you may find yourself fellowshipping with other believers, visiting other assemblies, or on vacation visiting another church. This is good in many ways, but keep in mind that you are to be "planted" in your home church/assembly where you serve, grow, support with time, talents, prayer, and finances. Just because you like another's style of preaching, ministering, or prophesying does not mean you uproot and move. Simply appreciate them but stay faithful to where God has planted you.

Those that be planted in the house of the Lord shall flourish in the courts of our God. They shall still bring forth fruit in old age; they shall be fat and flourishing; To shew that the Lord is upright: he is my rock, and there is no unrighteousness in him. (Psalm 92:13–15)

Let us hold fast the profession of our faith without wavering; (for he is faithful that promised;) And let us consider one another to provoke unto love and to good works: Not forsaking the assembling of ourselves together, as the manner of some is; but exhorting one another:

and so much the more, as ye see the day
approaching. (Hebrews 10:23–25)

With other believers (exhorting one another daily)

Take heed, brethren, lest there be in any
of you an evil heart of unbelief, in depart-
ing from the living God But exhort one
another daily, while it is called To day;
lest any of you be hardened through the
deceitfulness of sin. (Hebrews 3:12–13)

It is good to have faithful, trustworthy Christian friends
that can encourage you, fellowship with you, and pray with
you (even one Christian friend is better than none). A good
believer will tell you the truth in love. Ask God to put the
right people in your life. Also, ask God for the discernment
and wisdom to know if they are there for a season or for a
lifetime—there is a difference.

Two are better than one; because they
have a good reward for their labour. For
if they fall, the one will lift up his fellow:
but woe to him that is alone when he fall-
eth; for he hath not another to help him
up. (Ecclesiastes 4:9–10)

Service of Love

Your service of love to the King

> Jesus said unto him, Thou shalt love the
> Lord thy God with all thy heart, and
> with all thy soul, and with all thy mind.
> This is the first and great commandment.
> (Matthew 22:37–38)

> But seek ye first the kingdom of God, and
> His righteousness; and all these things
> shall be added unto you. (Matthew 6:3)

Our lives belong to God. We are not our own. Our priority should always be to God first, then to take care of our self, and then others.

> What? know ye not that your body is
> the temple of the Holy Ghost which is
> in you, which ye have of God, and ye are
> not your own? For ye are bought with a
> price: therefore glorify God in your body,
> and in your spirit, which are God's. (1
> Corinthians 6:19–20)

Your service of love to yourself

You are a three-part being: spirit, soul, and body. The Bible declares that at the point of salvation.

> This is the first and great commandment.
> And the second is like unto it, Thou shalt
> love thy neighbour as thyself. (Matthew
> 22:38–39)

You cannot biblically take care of your neighbor until you first take care of yourself. If you get sick and die, it will do no one any good. Personal care should be a priority. Then you will be healthy enough to serve, give, and love others. Please note in the verse below that your prosperity and health are related to you soul health.

> Beloved, I wish above all things that thou
> mayest prosper and be in health, even as
> thy soul prospereth. (3 John 1:2)

It is just as important to take care of your soul (mind, will, emotions) as it is to take care of your physical body. Things like a healthy self-esteem, a healthy perspective of yourself as defined by God, etc.

> For I say, through the grace given unto
> me, to every man that is among you,
> not to think of himself more highly than
> he ought to think; but to think soberly,
> according as God hath dealt to every man
> the measure of faith. (Romans 12:3)

Your service of love to the body of Christ

Some (not all) are called and mandated by God to minister unto the body of Christ. There are three types of servants/service to the body of Christ in general that I will discuss briefly here:

1. The first group—the Fivefold, the scriptures, tell us that this group are specifically chosen by Jesus himself which he gives to the body of believers as gifts. These, according to Ephesians 4:11, are apostles, prophets, evangelists, pastors, and teachers. This group of leaders are appointed by God and confirmed by the church presbytery. If they are ever self-appointed, that would be a counterfeit or a rebellious person acting out of order, or usurping persons, or those operating in witchcraft (like persons operating under the spirit of Jezebel).

2. The second group—other leadership persons such as administrators, assistants, armor bearers, ministry chairpersons like elders and deacons, gifts of government, etc. This group are very much needed and appreciated for what they contribute to the body of Christ in a local assembly or ministry. Although not one of the fivefold, they are still a very valuable and necessary assets to the body of believers, often working behind the scenes to help keep things running smoothly.

3. The third group—other lay persons, volunteers, helpers, committee persons, nursery workers, janitors, parking lot attendants, and a host of others. Again, these are often working behind the scenes. Although not in the limelight, they are very neces-

sary and greatly appreciated. Not often recognized for the time and effort they put in, yet a mature person will realize that their reward truly is with God and not man anyway. They should never be looked down upon or despised. An occasional sincere word of appreciation and thanks will go a long way to encourage them in their serving.

But quite the contrary, the parts of the body that seem to be weaker are [absolutely] necessary; and as for those parts of the body which we consider less honorable, these we treat with greater honor; and our less presentable parts are treated with greater modesty, while our more presentable parts do not require it. But God has combined the [whole] body, giving greater honor to that part which lacks it, so that there would be no division or discord in the body [that is, lack of adaptation of the parts to each other], but that the parts may have the same concern for one another. (1 Corinthians 12:22–25, AMP)

Your service of love to others

You may have other people in your sphere of influence that you are called to serve such as relatives, friends, neighbors, etc. Your service to them could be as simple as just loving, praying, or encouraging them. If you are married, you are called to minister to your spouse and children if you have any. In any case, prayer asking for God's grace to minister correctly, efficiently, and effectively is suggested.

Testimony

And they overcame him by the blood of
the Lamb, and by the word of their testimony; and they loved not their lives unto
the death. (Revelation 12:11)

Your testimony. Your personal testimony—no one can refute it!

No one ever lived your life, walked in your shoes, or
experienced what you went through. Your testimony is
unique to you. Your testimony can be simple yet very pow-
erful. How did you find Christ? Receive salvation? Get delivered from your mess and sins? Write it down; rehearse it. You
may need to share it at some point, to inspire faith, hope, or
inspire them to believe in God or what God can do.

Your testimony helps others

Some others may be more readily able to receive (the
gospel, salvation, healing, miracles, etc.) after you shared
what God did for you, saying within themselves, "If God did
it for you, he can do it for me!" At other times, you may be
able to share a portion of your personal testimony to minister
to and/or bring comfort to others so that they can understand and receive God's ministry to and for them.

Your testimony witnesses to the goodness and grace/mercy of God

In all rights, many of us would have been dead if it were not for the mercy of God! Many were in sin(s) that would have eventually killed you, but for the grace of God! Sin by nature itself will lead to death (physically and spiritually). But God, in his divine love and mercy, made a way for us to be delivered from sin and its bondage, making a way for us to be redeemed and saved through Christ Jesus.

When I got saved, my life changed drastically. I could not do any longer those things that I did before I got save. The drastic change in my life was so noticeable that three months later, my husband said, "You've changed. You're not the same woman I married!" So I asked him if the change was a good thing. He responded at the time, "I don't know. I haven't figured it out yet."

Nevertheless, I continued to study scriptures and pursue God with all my heart. It was not always easy living with an unsaved husband, but God gave me the grace I needed at the time. It wasn't until many years later that my husband also got saved. So I did what I could in the meantime and took the children to church myself, raised them, and taught them about God the best I knew how. They are all saved and filled with the Spirit now. Glory to God!

Your life an open book (epistle)

You do not live in a "bubble" totally isolated from the world. People are watching you: your family is watching you, your coworkers and/or classmates are watching you, you're neighbors and townspeople who see you on a regular basis are watching you. They are looking to see if you are a legitimate Christian, and how Christ has affected your life! Your life should reflect the attributes of Christ and how Jesus responded to situations. How did he live his life; better yet, how would he want you to live yours? Are you showing the people that are watching you that Jesus condones sin? Or are you living your life in holiness to the best of your ability, that others may see that you are an overcomer through God? So live your life to bring glory to our God and King in all that you say and do.

I know others have watched my Christian walk for many years, and some of them are now saved as a result of my consistent living and prayers for them. (How do I know? Because some have come to me and told me so.) Some have watched for twenty, twenty-five, and thirty-plus years; but now they are saved as a result, by the grace of God! Keep living right and holy; keep praying because you never know who is watching or how long it will take before they accept Jesus as Lord and Savior.

> Ye are our epistle written in our hearts, known and read of all men: Forasmuch as ye are manifestly declared to be the epistle of Christ ministered by us, written not with ink, but with the Spirit of the living God; not in tables of stone, but in fleshy tables of the heart. (2 Corinthians 3:2–3)

Witness

But ye shall receive power, after that the Holy Ghost is come upon you: and ye shall be witnesses unto me both in Jerusalem, and in all Judaea, and in Samaria, and unto the uttermost part of the earth. (Acts 1:8)

Your life that brings glory to Christ

You don't have to be an evangelist to be a witness. Everyone is a witness. You are witnesses of God's goodness, mercy, grace, salvation, and so on. Our very lives testify that God is gracious and merciful. As you live a pure life before God, your life will automatically testify (as stated before, you are an epistle written not with ink, but by God in your heart). Living your life should reflect the kingdom of God within you.

Your witnessing to others (evangelism)

Okay, so maybe you're not called to be an evangelist, but if you truly have tasted that God is good, I am sure at the very least you'll want your loved ones to be saved.

If God gives you opportunity to talk to your loved ones about salvation, then by all means do! Not all your loved ones are ready for that though. So at the very minimum, you can continue to pray for them.

I recommended that you pray for wisdom for yourself and ask God to help you to know what to say, when to say, when to be quiet, and when to just pray. You could possibly turn people off to God by being too overly zealous and forceful with them, trying to "cram Jesus down their throat." That is why I suggested praying for the wisdom, discernment, and timing to speak to those you're trying to lead to Christ. If you experience any resistance, perhaps that's the time to back off and keep praying versus openly trying to be forceful. God will give you the discernment and the grace you need if you ask him.

If they (your loved ones or ones you're witnessing to) are totally not going to hear anything you have to say, then pray that God will continue to work in their hearts, removing all excuses, and put other messengers in their path that will be able to speak to them in a way that they can receive.

Some plant seeds, some water, some harvest

> I have planted, Apollos watered; but God gave the increase. So then neither is he that planteth any thing, neither he that watereth; but God that giveth the increase. (1 Corinthians 3:6–7)

We sow "seeds" every time we talk to someone about God or tell someone about how or what God did for us and/or outright share the Gospel with someone. Planting, watering, or reaping a harvest (i.e., leading someone to Christ) are all important, yet different functions. This is done in faith, trusting God for their salvation. It may not be you, but another, that actually leads them to Christ. It may not even be in your lifetime, but if you prayed believing, and/or planted seeds by what you say, pray, and by the way you live, you can trust God to bring the increase as he sees fit. Believe me, you do your part, and God will do the rest! God is faithful and trustworthy.

Benefits of Salvation in Christ Jesus

And the greatest of these is love.

There are many benefits of being a Christian and living a Christian life. I am in no way claiming that this is an exhaustive list. This book was written to compile many of those benefits so that as a Christian, you could see and be made aware of some of the benefits we have and hold dear. In so doing, it is also my sincere hope that it will also build faith and hope in you. Knowing that God wants to bless us, reward us, and take care of us, as he is a good Father and a Good Shepherd toward us. God is not a hard taskmaster as some would suppose, but a loving Father that wants to bless His children. (Nevertheless, God also has standards by which we are to live, not excusing sin, but expecting us to live holy, clean, and righteous before him.)

> The law of the LORD is perfect, convert-
> ing the soul: the testimony of the LORD
> is sure, making wise the simple. The stat-

utes of the LORD are right, rejoicing the heart: *the commandment of the LORD* is pure, enlightening the eyes. The fear of the LORD is clean, enduring for ever: the judgments of the LORD are true and righteous altogether. More to be desired are *they* than gold, yea, than much fine gold: sweeter also than honey and the honeycomb. Moreover *by them* is thy servant warned: and in keeping of them there is *great reward*. (Psalm 19:7–11; emphasis added)

But without faith it is impossible to please him: for he that cometh to God must believe that he is, and that *he is a rewarder of them that diligently seek him.* (Hebrews 11:6; emphasis added)

Forgiveness of Sins

The difference between many other religions and God's kingdom is that he (God) has made provision for complete forgiveness of sins, once and for all of eternity. Whereas other religions have a "works" mentality, believing that you have to earn favor with their so-called deity, yet they fail to provide a way for sin to be forgiven or dealt with permanently.

Provision for forgiveness of sin(s), and being restored to right fellowship with our Creator, is one of our greatest benefits of becoming a Christian. As heirs of salvation, through the blood of Jesus Christ, we now live knowing that our sins have been paid for, and we are now free to live in right relationship with our God on his terms. (More on right relationship with God, see "Right Standing with God.")

There is great peace in knowing our sins have been forgiven by God.

> In whom we have redemption through his blood, the forgiveness of sins, according to the riches of his grace. (Ephesians 1:7)

> Who hath delivered us from the power of darkness, and hath translated us into the kingdom of his dear Son: In whom we have redemption through his blood, even the forgiveness of sins. (Colossians 1:13–14)

And you, being dead in your sins and
the uncircumcision of your flesh, hath
he quickened (made alive) together with
him, having forgiven you all trespasses.
(Colossians 2:13)

New Creation in Christ

Therefore if any man be in Christ, he is a new creature: old things are passed away; behold, all things are become new. And all things are of God, who hath reconciled us to himself by Jesus Christ, and hath given to us the ministry of reconciliation; To wit, that God was in Christ, reconciling the world unto himself, not imputing their trespasses unto them; and hath committed unto us the word of reconciliation. (2 Corinthians 5:17–18)

When you were "born again/anew" in Christ Jesus, the scriptures declare that you were made a new creature. "Old things" things of your past (sins, sinful behaviors or actions) no longer exist in the sight of God. As far as God is concerned, your past record was wiped clean (Colossians 2:13–14). Don't let the enemy or anyone else try to remind you of your former life, sins, failures, etc.

One of the tactics of the enemy is to directly or indirectly use people to try to bring shame, low self-esteem, guilt, or any other form of condemnation to try to make you feel bad about yourself so that you never reach your fullest potential and of your God-given call/destiny in Christ.

God forgives and gives you a new life. Live your life in the light of your new "grace" that God gives you.

Right Standing with God

Our right standing with God (our righteousness) is not anything of our own doing. Sin separated us from God's presence and holiness.

> Now then we are ambassadors for Christ, as though God did beseech you by us: we pray you in Christ's stead, be ye reconciled to God. For he hath made him to be sin for us, who knew no sin; that we might be made the righteousness of God in him. (2 Corinthians 5:18–19)

Understand this one thing, that we do not have any righteousness of our own. Through the sin passed on to us from the first Adam, we were unable to live perfectly holy (God's standard). Sin entered the world and disqualified and separated us from right relationship/fellowship with God.

> For all have sinned and fall short of the Glory of God. (Romans 3:23)

The only way for us to be restored in right relationship with God is for our sins/shortcomings to be remove out of the way. God is holy and cannot look upon sin. So in his infinite wisdom, he made provision for us, through his ultimate sacrifice—the holy, sinless blood and sacrifice of our Savior Christ Jesus to pay for our sins, once and for all. A divine transfer has been made. Our righteousness is now become that *of Jesus's* (by his precious blood that was shed for us which was applied to our account when we receive him at our point of our salvation). It is a gift of God and not of our own works. A precious gift that cannot be earned or deserved, given by the love and grace of our heavenly Father in true love for each and every one of us.

> But we are all as an unclean thing, and all our righteousnesses are as filthy rags; and we all do fade as a leaf; and our iniquities, like the wind, have taken us away. (Isaiah 64:6)

> As it is written, There is none righteous, no, not one. (Romans 3:10)

> For by grace are ye saved through faith; and that not of yourselves: it is the gift of God: Not of works, lest any man should boast. (Ephesians 2:8–9)

This is the "great exchange." We could not do it ourselves, we could not save ourselves, but when we received his sacrifice for us at salvation, his blood was applied to us and we were forgiven all, and his righteousness was applied to us that moment of our salvation. We now stand before him covered in his blood, holy, forgiven, and righteousness.

> Even the righteousness of God which is by faith of Jesus Christ unto all and upon

all them that believe: for there is no difference: For all have sinned, and come
short of the glory of God; Being justified
freely by his grace through the redemption that is in Christ Jesus: Whom
God hath set forth to be a propitiation
through faith in his blood, to declare his
righteousness for the remission of sins
that are past, through the forbearance
of God; To declare, I say, at this time his
righteousness: that he might be just, and
the justifier of him which believeth in
Jesus. (Romans 3:22–26)

Note in terminology: Being made righteous (right standing with God) has been given to us as explained in the above
scriptures. However, "living righteous" is about your behavior, character, and integrity, how you conduct yourselves in
your everyday lives. We should as "Christ-ians" exhibit his
love, mercy, forgiveness, holiness, strength, and compassion,
living holy, pure, and clean before him. (See also Romans
12:1–3.)

Curses Broken

Curses are results of sin, disobedience, or wrong behavior, whether done by you or by a bloodline relative, the penalty of which is passed on to you and/or your children, grandchildren, and great-grandchildren.

> Thou shalt not bow down thyself to them, nor serve them: for I the Lord thy God am a jealous God, visiting the iniquity of the fathers upon the children unto the third and fourth generation of them that hate me; And shewing mercy unto thousands of them that love me, and keep my commandments. (Exodus 20:5–6)

The enemy of our soul is a legalist. If he can get away with it, he will keep perpetuating ill against you. This may include, but not limited to sin, sickness, disease, infirmity, and generational weaknesses that result in vulnerabilities to lust, sin, etc. Things like divorce, stroke, fornication, adultery, etc., could be signs of generational curses. Have you ever noticed when you visit a doctor, one of the first thing that they ask you about is your family history? Is there heart disease? Asthma? Diabetes? Whether or not they realize it, they know the principle that some of these illness and diseases "run" in the family line. From a biblical perspective, we know them to be generational curses (Exodus 20:5).

The good news is that now that you are a Christian, Jesus took *all* the payment for your sin, your past and all the past legal evidences (handwritings) against you and your bloodline, and provided the sacrifice acceptable to God (the qualifying payment) for your redemption and nailed it to the cross—"Paid in full," Jesus declared on the cross.

> And you, being dead in your sins and the uncircumcision of your flesh, hath he quickened together with him, having forgiven you all trespasses; Blotting out the handwriting of ordinances that was against us, which was contrary to us, and took it out of the way, nailing it to his cross. (Colossians 2:13–14)

> Christ hath redeemed us from the curse of the law, being made a curse for us: for it is written, cursed is every one that hangeth on a tree. (Galatians 3:13)

> When Jesus therefore had received the vinegar, he said, It is finished (the payment is completed): and he bowed his head, and gave up the ghost. (John 19:30)

That payment for sins and curses was applied to your account (once and for all) when you accepted God's salvation through Christ Jesus. You are forgiven! And no one can accuse you of your past (pre-Christian life) ever again. As far as God is concerned, it was blotted out—no more record of it. You have been pardoned!

So the next time the enemy or anyone else tries to remind you of your past (or that of a bloodline/generational curse), tell him there is nothing valid any more on record, and quote the following scripture (*the scriptures speaking of the work of Christ Jesus on the cross*):

> Blotting out the handwriting of ordinances that was against us, which was contrary to us, and took it out of the way, nailing it to his cross. And having spoiled principalities and powers, he made a shew of them openly, triumphing over them in it. (Colossians 2:14–15)

So what happens if I accidently sin again?

> If we say that we have fellowship with him, and walk in darkness, we lie, and do not the truth: But if we walk in the light, as he is in the light, we have fellowship one with another, and the blood of Jesus Christ his Son cleanseth us from all sin. If we say that we have no sin, we deceive ourselves, and the truth is not in us. If we confess our sins, he is faithful and just to forgive us our sins, and to cleanse us from all unrighteousness. If we say that we have not sinned, we make him a liar, and his word is not in us. (1 John 1:6–10)

> My little children, these things write I
> unto you, that ye sin not. And if any man
> sin, we have an advocate with the Father,
> Jesus Christ the righteous: And he (Jesus)
> is the propitiation* for our sins: and not
> for ours only, but also for the sins of the
> whole world. (1 John 2:1–2)

"*Haiasmos*" is atonement that is (concretely) an expiator: propitiation.

"Expiator"—to make amends or reparation for; atone for: expiate one's sins by acts of penance. v. intr. To make amends; atone. [Latin *expiāre, expiāt-* : ex-, intensive pref.; see ex- + *piāre*, to atone (from pious, devout).]

Jesus not only loves us, saves, and redeems us, but is also qualified to forgive us and cleanse us from unrighteousness if we sincerely repent and ask forgiveness.

Jesus also is at the right hand of God, is constantly praying for us, and is in agreement with God's divine purpose for our lives.

> Who is he that condemneth? It is Christ
> that died, yea rather, that is risen again,
> who is even at the right hand of God,
> who also maketh intercession for us.
> (Romans 8:34)

> By so much was Jesus made a surety of
> a better testament. And they truly were

---

* Propitiation—G2435, Strong's Concordance = "*hilasterion*" (hil-as-tay'-ree-on); an expiatory (place or thing) that is (concretely) an atoning victim or (specifically) the lid of the Ark (in the temple); mercy seat, propitiation.

> many priests, because they were not suf-
> fered to continue by reason of death:
> But this man, because he continueth
> ever, hath an unchangeable priesthood.
> Wherefore he is able also to save them
> to the uttermost that come unto God by
> him, seeing he ever liveth to make inter-
> cession for them. (Hebrews 7:22–25)

In the scriptures above, "intercession" is the word—
G1793, Strong's Concordance = "*entugchano*" (en-toong-
khan'-o); to chance upon that is by implication confer with;
by extension to entreat (in favor for or against); deal with,
make intercession.

God knows our very thoughts and motives. He knows
when we've made a mistake and when we are sincere about
repenting. You cannot fool God. You would only be fooling
yourself if you're not honest or sincere when it comes to the
things of God. So things like denial, deception, attempts to
cover up a (sin/sinful) matters, and/or other lying maneuvers
of contrition to try to justify iniquity/sin are useless. God
desires truth in our heart/our inner parts.

> Behold, thou desirest truth in the inward
> parts: and in the hidden part thou shalt
> make me to know wisdom. (Psalm 51:6)

Adopted by the Father

God the Father loves us so much that he does not treat us like castaways, slaves, or nobodies. He loves us so much that he personally has adopted us into his family and desires a close relationship and fellowship with us (on his terms, in right standing with him.)

> For ye have not received the spirit of bondage again to fear; but ye have received the Spirit of adoption, whereby we cry, Abba, Father. (Romans 8:15)

> But when the fulness of the time was come, God sent forth his Son, made of a woman, made under the law, To redeem them that were under the law, that we might receive the adoption of sons. And because ye are sons, God hath sent forth the Spirit of his Son into your hearts, crying, Abba, Father. (Galatians 4:4–6)

> According as he hath chosen us in him before the foundation of the world, that we should be holy and without blame before him in love: Having predestinated us unto the adoption of children by Jesus

Christ to himself, according to the good pleasure of his will, To the praise of the glory of his grace, wherein he hath made us accepted in the beloved. (Ephesians 1:4–6)

New Citizenship

A divine transfer of citizenship was made when you were saved (born again, born anew.) Your citizenship on this earth was transferred from the kingdom of darkness (this world's system and its rulers) to the kingdom of God (the eternal, heavenly kingdom and its ruler, the only King of kings and Lord of lords). We are now foreigners and sojourners on this earth, as ambassadors of the kingdom of God, until the appointed time that God calls us home.

> Now therefore ye are no more strangers and foreigners, but, fellowcitizens with the saints, and of the household of God (Ephesians 2:19)

> Who hath delivered us from the power of darkness, and hath translated us into the kingdom of his dear Son. (Colossians 1:13)

Although we are human and live on the earth, for a specified period, that time is temporary and relatively short in comparison to eternity. While we are here on earth, we are to abide by the laws of the land wherever possible. For example, when we travel to another nation (like from the USA to Europe or from Japan to Australia) we must abide by the laws of the nation we visit, but our citizenship remains in our "home" country. So too, as we continue our journey here on earth, we are to abide by the laws of the land where we reside. Yet our new citizenship is now of the kingdom of God. We are now ambassadors and citizens of God's kingdom and the rules and laws of the divine heavenly kingdom are those of which now govern our lives.

While we are here, we are to respect the laws of the land *and* pray for those in authority here on earth (Jeremiah 29:7) that we may live in peace here until "that Day" when God takes us home.

> I exhort therefore, that, first of all, supplications, prayers, intercessions, and giving of thanks, be made for all men; For kings, and for all that are in authority; that we may lead a quiet and peaceable life in all godliness and honesty. For this is good and acceptable in the sight of God our Saviour. (1 Timothy 2:1–3)

Deliverance from Egypt (Bondage of Sin)

For the law of the Spirit of life in Christ
Jesus hath made me free from the law of
sin and death. (Romans 8:2)

When we were in the world (pre-salvation in Jesus), we were in bondage to sin and the effects/penalties of sin. After your salvation experience, you are now legally free from the power of and from the bondage of those sins (yours and any bloodline or generational curses that may have transferred to you. (See section on "Curses Broken" in this book.)

The children's bread (deliverance)

Bread is a basic staple in most people's diet. So it goes to say that deliverance has been provided as one of the basic staples available to us as Christians (and in some rare cases for the unsaved too, usually for the purposes of leading them unto salvation).

However, for some, not everyone, it is possible that you may have picked up a demon or two, or a few along your journey in life (as a result of your behavior, actions, choices, sins of the fathers, or a trauma of some sort, wrong associations, soul ties, etc.). In which case, provision has been made available to you to be made free from them (and/or to have them removed.)

There is nothing to be ashamed of. If you are a child of God and need help to remove the now "trespasser" in your life, then love yourself enough to seek out help from an anointed, skilled man or woman of God who knows how to do deliverance and get free from those trespassers once and for all. It's your right and privilege as a child of God.

> And, behold, a woman of Canaan came out of the same coasts, and cried unto him, saying, Have mercy on me, O Lord, thou son of David; my daughter is grievously vexed with a devil. But he answered her not a word. And his disciples came and besought him, saying, Send her away; for she crieth after us. But he answered and said, I am not sent but unto the lost sheep of the house of Israel. Then came she and worshipped him, saying, Lord, help me. But he answered and said, It is not meet to take *the children's bread*, and to cast it to dogs. And she said, Truth, Lord: yet the dogs eat of the crumbs which fall from their masters' table. Then Jesus answered and said unto her, O woman, great is thy faith: be it unto thee even as thou wilt. And her daughter was made whole from that very hour. (Matthew 15:22–28; emphasis added)

Blessed
Covenant Blessings to Us

A great and precious promise was made to Abraham (and indirectly to us who are now Christians). We inherit the blessings of Abraham as we through Christ have become his descendants.

> Know ye therefore that they which are of faith, the same are the children of Abraham. And the scripture, foreseeing that God would justify the heathen through faith, preached before the gospel unto Abraham, saying, In thee shall all nations be blessed. So then they which be of faith *are blessed* with faithful Abraham. (Galatians 3:7–9; see also Genesis 22:16–18)

> The Spirit itself beareth witness with our spirit, that we are the children of God: And if children, then heirs; heirs of God, and joint heirs with Christ; if so be that we suffer with him, that we may be also glorified together. (Romans 8:17)

Rewards—Now and in Heaven

Great Reward

Jesus said, "If you love me, you will keep my commandments." We see that there is great reward attached to the keeping of God's commandments, laws, testimonies, statutes, etc. They are literally more valuable than fine gold.

> The law of the LORD is perfect, converting the soul: the testimony of the LORD is sure, making wise the simple. The statutes of the LORD are right, rejoicing the heart: the commandment of the LORD_is pure, enlightening the eyes. The fear of the LORD is clean, enduring for ever: the judgments of the LORD are true and righteous altogether. More to be desired are they than gold, yea, than much fine gold: sweeter also than honey and the honeycomb. Moreover by them is thy servant warned: and in keeping of them there is *great reward*. (Psalm 19:7–11; emphasis added)

Crowns

Many crowns are given in scripture to those who are faithful and/or faithfully serve God. They are blessings given to those who qualify. These crowns would not have been obtained if God did not create and save us in the first place (Romans 11:35–36, below). This keeps us from attitudes of entitlement and being lifted in pride. After all, he is the one who created us, saved us, and blesses us out of his eternal love and holiness. We are nothing without him! The twenty-four elders before the throne in Revelation 4:10–11 (below) exhibit this for us in true adoration, thankfulness, gratefulness, gratitude, and humility, as they lay (cast) their crowns down before the feet of Jesus and worship him.

> The four and twenty elders fall down before him that sat on the throne, and worship him that liveth for ever and ever, and cast their crowns before the throne, saying, Thou art worthy, O Lord, to receive glory and honour and power: for thou hast created all things, and for thy pleasure they are and were created. (Revelation 4:10–11)

> Or who hath first given to him, and it shall be recompensed unto him again? For of him, and through him, and to him, are all things: to whom be glory for ever. Amen. (Romans 11:35–36)

Some of the crowns mentioned in the Bible are:
1. The Crown of Life—Revelation 2:10
    For those who remain steadfast through trials and/
    or have suffered for Christ.
2. The Incorruptible Crown—1 Corinthians 9:25
    For those who show self-control, moderation, and
    live faithfully.
3. The Crown of Righteousness—2 Timothy 4:8
    For those who live their lives anticipating the second coming of Christ.
4. The Crown of Glory—1 Peter 5:2–4
    For those who instruct others in God's Word.
5. The Crown of Rejoicing—1 Thessalonians 2:19
    For those who win souls.

Rewards now and in heaven

Rewards can be received both now and in heaven.

The disciples where concerned because they gave up businesses, houses, etc. to serve the Lord. When they expressed their concerns, Jesus gave them a great and precious promise:

> And every one that hath forsaken houses, or brethren, or sisters, or father, or mother, or wife, or children, or lands, for my name's sake, shall receive an hundredfold, and shall inherit everlasting life. (Matthew 19:29)

> And Jesus answered and said, Verily I say unto you, There is no man that hath left house, or brethren, or sisters, or father,

or mother, or wife, or children, or lands, for my sake, and the gospel's, But he shall receive an hundredfold *now in this time*, houses, and brethren, and sisters, and mothers, and children, and lands, with persecutions; and *in the world to come* eternal life. (Mark 10:29–30; emphasis added)

In the above scriptures, we see that a "hundredfold" return is promised in this time for those things that we gave up to serve the Lord and that the inheritance of everlasting life is also promised in the world to come. This is a win-win proposition. We win now, and we win later.

Treasures. Many treasures are promised to those who will seek the wisdom and understanding of God. Promise of riches, honor, righteousness, substance, and treasures are named among them in Proverbs 8:12–21.

I wisdom (of God) dwell with prudence, and find out knowledge of witty inventions. The fear of the Lord is to hate evil: pride, and arrogancy, and the evil way, and the froward mouth, do I hate. Counsel is mine, and sound wisdom: I am understanding; I have strength. By me kings reign, and princes decree justice. By me princes rule, and nobles, even all the judges of the earth. I love them that love me; and those that seek me early shall find me. Riches and honour are with me; yea, durable riches and righteousness. My fruit is better than gold, yea, than fine gold; and my revenue than choice silver. I lead in the way of righteousness, in the midst of the paths of judgment: That I may cause those that love me to *inherit substance*; and *I will fill their treasures*. (Proverbs 8:12–21; emphasis added)

Unique treasures. In Colossians 2:3 below, we see that treasures are not just money or substance (material items), but also things like understanding, wisdom, knowledge, and revelation of the mysteries of God (see "Riches of God's Mysteries Revealed" in this book).

That their hearts might be comforted, being knit together in love, and unto all riches of the full assurance of understanding, to the acknowledgement of the mystery of God, and of the Father, and of Christ; 3 In whom are hid all the treasures of wisdom and knowledge. (Colossians 2:3)

Hidden treasures. Treasures can be hidden, secret, out of view or grasp for most. However, God has said that he would reveal, expose, and give these hidden treasures to his people. God will use many of these treasures to confirm his sovereignty and to be a testament to him directly.

And I will give thee the treasures of darkness, and hidden riches of secret places, that thou mayest know that I, the LORD,

which call thee by thy name, am the God
of Israel. (Isaiah 45:3)

Treasure in heaven. Scriptures tell us that we have the opportunity and privilege of laying up treasure for ourselves in heaven. The Word of God also tells us how. In Matthew 6:20–21 and Mark 10:21 below, Jesus himself says that you can "lay up" treasures in heaven that are protected from corruption, rust, and theft.

> But lay up for yourselves treasures in heaven, where neither moth nor rust doth corrupt, and where thieves do not break through nor steal: For where your treasure is, there will your heart be also. (Matthew 6:20–21)

Creating our personal heavenly bank accounts are explained in the scriptures above and below. Scripturally, the way that you can get treasures in heaven for your account is explained in the Word by the act of giving to the poor; helping those in need that cannot pay you back; and taking care of the poor, maimed, lame, and blind (Matt. 6:20–21, Luke 18:22, Mark 12:33–34, and Luke 14:13–14)

> Then Jesus beholding him loved him, and said unto him, One thing thou lackest: go thy way, sell whatsoever thou hast, and give to the poor, and thou shalt have treasure in heaven: and come, take up the cross, and follow me. (Mark 10:21)

> Sell that ye have, and give alms; provide yourselves bags which wax not old, a treasure in the heavens that faileth not, where no thief approacheth, neither moth corrupteth. For where your treasure is, there will your heart be also. (Mark 12:33–34)

> But when thou makest a feast, call the poor, the maimed, the lame, the blind: And thou shalt be blessed; for they cannot recompense thee: for thou shalt be recompensed at the resurrection of the just. (Luke 14:13–14)

Although giving to the poor is important, it is a worthless effort if you do not develop a relationship with Jesus. A close relationship with Jesus should be our number 1 priority. This close relationship with the Son of God should be the foundation through which all other activity and responses flow. Even our declared love for him means nothing if we don't first get to *know* him (intimacy in relationship—not the sexual kind, but the closeness as of dearest friends).

> Not every one that saith unto me, Lord, Lord, shall enter into the kingdom of heaven; but he that doeth the will of my Father which is in heaven. Many will say to me in that day, Lord, Lord, have we not prophesied in thy name? and in thy name have cast out devils? and in thy name done many wonderful works? And then will I profess unto them, I never

knew you: depart from me, ye that work
iniquity. (Matthew 7:20–22)

Treasure on earth (now). Throughout scripture, there
are many examples of those who followed hard after God,
with persistence and sincerity of heart (lip service does not
qualify you). Through many tests, trials, and temptations,
those in the scriptures have consistently proven their love and
devotion for God by their *actions* and obedience. And God
rewarded them accordingly.

> Talk no more so exceeding proudly; let
> not arrogancy come out of your mouth:
> for the LORD is a God of knowledge, and
> by him *actions* are weighed. (1 Samuel
> 2:3; emphasis added)

Some examples below from scriptures are:
Abraham—both Abraham's heart and faith were tested
by the Lord God, when God asked Abraham to sacrifice his
promised, beloved son. As Abraham obeyed, God responded
with the following blessing:

> And said, By myself have I sworn, saith
> the Lord, for because thou hast done this
> thing, and hast not withheld thy son,
> thine only son: That in blessing I will bless
> thee, and in multiplying I will multiply
> thy seed as the stars of the heaven, and as
> the sand which is upon the sea shore; and
> thy seed shall possess the gate of his ene-
> mies; And in thy seed shall all the nations

of the earth be blessed; because thou hast
obeyed my voice. (Genesis 22:16–18)

Moses—born an Israelite, raised in the courts of pharaoh of Egypt. Moses was taught and trained as a warrior, ruler, leader, and king. He learned to read, write, war, and govern as a king (a pharaoh's protégé and potential heir to the throne). God used him to deliver and preserve the Hebrews from slavery and bondage, gave them God's laws and ordinances through Moses's hand, and later to lead them up to the Promised Land.

Though he made some mistakes, Moses was still God's choice for many tasks. We even see God the Father using Moses and Elijah to counsel Jesus in the New Testament at the mount of transfiguration (a testament of eternal life and of heaven's eternal kingdom that supersedes anything in the earth realm).

And there appeared unto them Elias with
Moses: and they were talking with Jesus.
(Mark 9:4) (For further studies on this,
see Hebrews 11:1–40.)

Throughout human history, God, in his infinite wisdom and grace, has shown himself a loving and generous sovereign. He is loving and giving by nature, his very essence is pure love. He loves to give, bless, and reward those who diligently seek and obey him.

But without faith it is impossible to
please him: for he that cometh to God
must believe that he is, and that he is a
rewarder of them that diligently seek him.

(Hebrews 11:6) (Note: It says, "them that diligently seek him," not him that seeks the riches or substance.)

For thou, Lord, wilt bless the righteous; with favour wilt thou compass him as with a shield. (Psalm 5:12)

In the house of the righteous is much treasure: but in the revenues of the wicked is trouble. (Proverbs 15:6)

[The wisdom of God speaks] That I may cause those that love me to inherit substance; and I will fill their treasures. (Proverbs 8:21)

And Jesus answered and said, Verily I say unto you, There is no man that hath left house, or brethren, or sisters, or father, or mother, or wife, or children, or lands, for my sake, and the gospel's, But he shall receive an hundredfold now in this time, houses, and brethren, and sisters, and mothers, and children, and lands, with persecutions; and in the world to come eternal life. (Mark 10:29–30)

Mind of Christ

Wisdom, knowledge, and counsel of God are available to us Christians through the mind of Christ. Insanity is never to be our portion. If someone is experiencing confusion, it is usually an attack against them, or something they are bringing on themselves as a result of being out of order or being in unrepentant sin. In these cases, warfare prayer or repentance, depending on the situation, can elevate the symptoms of the confusion.

God's wisdom, direction, heart on matters, and understanding are available to us if we would only ask him in faith and be still and listen.

> For who hath known the mind of the Lord, that he may instruct him? but we have the mind of Christ. (1 Corinthians 2:16)

> For God hath not given us the spirit of fear; but of power, and of love, and of a sound mind. (2 Timothy 1:7)

> Be still, and know that I am God: I will be exalted among the heathen, I will be exalted in the earth. (Psalm 46:10)

> If any of you lack wisdom, let him ask of God, that giveth to all men liberally, and upbraideth not; and it shall be given him. But let him ask in faith, nothing wavering. For he that wavereth is like a wave of the sea driven with the wind and tossed. For let not that man think that he shall receive any thing of the Lord. (James 1:5–7)

Riches of God's Mysteries Revealed

Riches also come to us as God reveals and unlocks his mysteries, enlightening our understanding that Christ in us is our hope of glory, which is the most treasured benefit of God's graciousness and a priceless gift to us Christians.

> Even the mystery which hath been hid from ages and from generations, but now is made manifest to his saints: To whom God would make known what is *the riches of the glory of this mystery* among the Gentiles; which is Christ in you, the hope of glory._(Colossians 1:26–27)

(Some other mysteries revealed: see Mark 4:11, Romans 11:25, 1 Corinthians 15:49–57, Ephesians 1:9–12, Ephesians3:3–6.)

Counsel of God

The counsel of God is available to us. God did not leave us to fend for ourselves, but made provision for us. His counsel is beyond that of natural man and is immutable.

> I will bless the LORD, who hath given me counsel: my reins also instruct me in the night seasons. (Psalm 16:7)

> The *counsel* of the LORD standeth for ever, the thoughts of his heart to all generations. (Psalm 33:11; emphasis added)

Thou shalt guide me with thy counsel, and afterward receive me to glory. (Psalm 73:24)

[Of the Messiah] And the spirit of the LORD shall rest upon him, the spirit of wisdom and understanding, the spirit of counsel and might, the spirit of knowledge and of the fear of the LORD. (Isaiah 11:2)

This also cometh forth from the LORD of hosts, which is wonderful in counsel, and excellent in working. (Isaiah 28:29)

Wherein God, willing more abundantly to shew unto the heirs of promise the immutability of his counsel, confirmed it by an oath. (Hebrews 6:17)

Access to the Throne of God

God is holy and cannot look on sin. Therefore, provision had to be made in order for us to have access to his throne with our petitions. Jesus's righteousness, which was applied to our account at the point of salvation, cleanses us from sin; and his blood that is ever on the mercy seat through which the Father sees us, still avails for us. (He no longer sees our sin, but the blood of his Son that still cries, "Holy, holy, holy," on our behalf. He now sees us through that blood.)

> For such an high priest [Jesus] became us, who is holy, harmless, undefiled, separate from sinners, and made higher than the heavens; Who needeth not daily, as those high priests, to offer up sacrifice, first for his own sins, and then for the people's: for this he did once, when he offered up himself. (Hebrews 7:26–27)

> Having therefore, brethren, boldness to enter into the holiest by the blood of Jesus. (Hebrews 10:19)

> According to the eternal purpose which he purposed in Christ Jesus our Lord: In whom we have boldness and access

with confidence by the faith of him.
(Ephesians 3:11–12)

Let us therefore come boldly unto the
throne of grace, that we may obtain
mercy, and find grace to help in time of
need. (Hebrews 4:16)

Therefore being justified by faith, we
have peace with God through our Lord
Jesus Christ: By whom also we have
access by faith into this grace wherein we
stand, and rejoice in hope of the glory of
God. (Romans 5:1–2)

God will never leave you

Many in life have experienced abandonment from a
parent, loved one, or some other(s). God promises in his
Word that he will never leave us or forsake us. He is not a
man that he lies, neither can he lie. Believe him when he said
it because he cannot lie!

God is one you can truly trust and rely on. He never
leaves us. If we are feeling that way (like "God has left me"),
it is not God who has left, but rather you who has pulled
back in some way. Check your heart, repent, ask for forgiveness, and get back into right fellowship with him. Worship
and pray until you can once again discern God's presence and
hear him clearly.

Let your conversation be without covet-
ousness; and be content with such things as

ye have: for he hath said, I will never leave thee, nor forsake thee. (Hebrews 13:5)

But Zion said, The LORD hath forsaken me, and my Lord hath forgotten me. Can a woman forget her sucking child, that she should not have compassion on the son of her womb? yea, they may forget, yet will I not forget thee. Behold, I have graven thee upon the palms of my hands; thy walls are continually before me. (Isaiah 49:14–16)

And I will pray the Father, and he shall give you another Comforter, that he may abide with you for ever. (John 14:16)

The Precious Holy Spirit of God

Holy Spirit is in *and* with *us*

Please don't misunderstand. The Holy Spirit is and has always been very much God, whether or not you received salvation. He will always be God, regardless of your (or anyone else's) salvation experience or lack thereof.

My intentions here are to show the integral workings and relationship of the Holy Spirit in the life of a Christian (one of our most treasured benefits). It is very important and necessary that you get to know and allow the Holy Spirit to work in your life. Your relationship with the Holy Spirit is essential to your growth, understanding, maturity. The Holy Spirit is and does provide a host of other benefits and necessities in the life of a Christian.

We can see and understand just a few of those benefits and necessities by looking at some of the names and at some of the attributes and functions of the Holy Spirit. (Note: Again, this is not a complete list. I recommend that you study it out further for more understanding.)

> Even the Spirit of truth; whom the world cannot receive, because it seeth him not, neither knoweth him: but ye know him; for he dwelleth with you, and shall be in you. (John 14:17)

Some names and attributes of the Holy Spirit

The Comforter.

> And I will pray the Father, and he shall give you another Comforter, that he may abide with you for ever. (John 14:16)

> But the Comforter, which is the Holy Ghost, whom the Father will send in my name, he shall teach you all things, and bring all things to your remembrance, whatsoever I have said unto you. (John 14:26)

> Nevertheless I tell you the truth; It is expedient for you that I go away: for if I go not away, the Comforter will not come unto you; but if I depart, I will send him unto you. (John 16:7)

Biblical definition of "comforter": *Comforter*—G3875, Strong's Concordance = *"parakletos"* (par-ak'-lay-tos); an intercessor, *consoler*, advocate, comforter.

Consoler—one who consoles.

Console—to alleviate or lessen the grief, sorrow, or disappointment of; give solace or comfort. (John 14:16, 26, John 15:26, John 16:7 all have the same word and definition for *comforter*.)

The Spirit of Truth. The Spirit of Truth can be totally trusted because he speaks the truth and does not lie, neither can he lie. He is holy. Every counsel from the Lord is for our benefit. He would never lead you astray. He lives with us and is in us, always there for us, and will never leave us. His truth is pure and enlightening. His wisdom is readily available to us (James 1:5–8). All we have to do is ask in faith.

> Even the Spirit of truth; whom the world cannot receive, because it seeth him not, neither knoweth him: but ye know him; for he dwelleth with you, and shall be in you. (John 14:17)

> But when the Comforter is come, whom I will send unto you from the Father, even the Spirit of truth, which proceedeth from the Father, he shall testify of me. (John 15:26)

> Howbeit when he, the Spirit of truth, is come, he will guide you into all truth: for he shall not speak of himself; but whatsoever he shall hear, that shall he speak: and he will shew you things to come. (John 16:13)

> God is not a man, that he should lie; neither the son of man, that he should repent: hath he said, and shall he not do it? or hath he spoken, and shall he not make it good? (Numbers 23:19)

The Spirit of Christ. The Spirit of Christ, another name for the Holy Spirit of God which reveals his origin as divinely related to Christ. We see he was working before creation, throughout history, during the life of Jesus, here on earth, and is with us even now.

The Spirit of Christ is sent by Jesus the Christ to be with us to comfort, guide, teach, and a host of other interactions with us. Being spirit, he is not limited to time, space, matter, or human frailty, such as a physical body. Therefore, he can be in all places at all times and is not limited as Jesus was in his incarnated body. Christ himself knew we would need another one to help us in our walk with God and sent the Holy Spirit to help.

> Searching what, or what manner of time the Spirit of Christ which was in them did signify, when it testified beforehand the sufferings of Christ, and the glory that should follow. (1 Peter 1:11)

> And I will pray the Father, and he shall give you another Comforter, that he may abide with you for ever. (John 14:16)

The Spirit of Holiness. It is no surprise that the Holy Spirit is holy! Even his name reveals this attribute and his very character and nature. His very essence is holy. If the Holy Spirit is God and is holy, we ought to treat him with all honor and with the utmost respect.

> And declared to be the Son of God with power, according to the spirit of holiness, by the resurrection from the dead. (Romans 1:4)

Some attributes and functions of the Holy Spirit

Teach.

> But the anointing which ye have received
> of him abideth in you, and ye need not
> that any man teach you: but as the same
> anointing teacheth you of all things, and
> is truth, and is no lie, and even as it hath
> taught you, ye shall abide in him. (1 John
> 2:27)

> But the Comforter, which is the Holy
> Ghost, whom the Father will send in my
> name, he shall teach you all things, and
> bring all things to your remembrance,
> whatsoever I have said unto you. (John
> 14:26)

Bring to remembrance words of Christ. The Holy Spirit
aids in remembering the Word of God. He knows how to
affect our memory and how to help us recall what we need
concerning his Word when we need it.

> But the Comforter, which is the Holy
> Ghost, whom the Father will send in my
> name, he shall teach you all things, and
> bring all things to your remembrance,
> whatsoever I have said unto you. (John
> 14:26)

Comfort and/or solace.

> But the Comforter, which is the Holy
> Ghost, whom the Father will send in my
> name, he shall teach you all things, and
> bring all things to your remembrance,
> whatsoever I have said unto you. (John
> 14:26)

As mentioned earlier (in this chapter, in the section referring to the names of the Holy Spirit), he is not only called the Comforter, but it is also what he does among many other things. In comforting, he also helps to alleviate or lessen grief, sorrow, or disappointment. Far too many people turn to carnal things to help bring comfort, such as food, sex, drugs, alcohol, and things like over-achieving, perfectionism, and other vices. If the Holy Spirit is our comforter, we can learn to go to him for help when we are stressed, sad, angry, frustrated, etc. His ways are perfect and will help us bringing comfort and/or solace without any of the adverse side effects that carnal means do. This swapping of God's comfort as opposed to the carnal means does not always happen overnight. Many times, it is a process that with consistent effort, will eventually payoff and become a great habit of replacement of the other detrimental devises.

Presents us before the throne faultless. The precious Holy Spirit will help clean us up. He is the one who will present us (the bride of Christ) before the throne of God faultless. The Holy Spirit will also help "keep" us from falling.

This work of the Holy Spirit in our lives is so vital and should be appreciated. We should honor and acknowledge him in it. I believe this is one of the reasons that we should never "grieve" the Holy Spirit or sin against him.

> Now unto him that is able to keep you from falling, and to present you fault-less before the presence of his glory with exceeding joy. (Jude 1:24)

> And grieve not the holy Spirit of God, whereby ye are sealed unto the day of redemption. (Ephesians 4:30)

> Wherefore I say unto you, All manner of sin and blasphemy shall be forgiven unto men: but the blasphemy against the Holy Ghost shall not be forgiven unto men. (Matthew 12:31)

Guide, lead, direct. The Spirit of God speaks to us and directs us in our daily lives if we would be sensitive enough to listen. Most of the time, he comes as a still small voice, a voice from behind you saying, "This is the way. Walk ye in it."

> Howbeit when he, the Spirit of truth, is come, he will guide you into all truth: for he shall not speak of himself; but whatso-ever he shall hear, that shall he speak: and he will shew you things to come. (John 16:13)

> And thine ears shall hear a word behind thee, saying, This is the way, walk ye in it, when ye turn to the right hand, and when ye turn to the left. (Isaiah 30:21)

My sheep hear my voice, and I know
them, and they follow me. (John 10:27)

Convict, convince, reprove, rebuke, chasten. The Holy
Spirit is the one who will convict sinners and saints alike. He
will bring rebuke when needed. He will chasten those whom
God has called to be his sons (heirs). Just as a loving parent
wants their child to do/be right, so God wants us to act right;
and as a loving Father, he will correct us by His Spirit.

And when he is come, he will reprove the
world of sin, and of righteousness, and
of judgment: Of sin, because they believe
not on me; Of righteousness, because I
go to my Father, and ye see me no more;
Of judgment, because the prince of this
world is judged. (John 16:8–11)

And ye have forgotten the exhorta-
tion which speaketh unto you as unto
children, My son, despise not thou the
chastening of the Lord, nor faint when
thou art rebuked of him: For whom the
Lord loveth he chasteneth, and scour-
geth every son whom he receiveth. If ye
endure chastening, God dealeth with you
as with sons; for what son is he whom the
father chasteneth not? But if ye be without chastisement, whereof all are partak-
ers, then are ye bastards, and not sons.
(Hebrews 12:5–8)

Gives wisdom, knowledge, understanding, revelation: The Spirit of God gives revelation, wisdom, and understanding in all things. If we don't understand, we are instructed to ask God who will give it to you liberally and upbraideth (scolds) not. So you don't ever have to feel ashamed to ask.

As believers, we readily have the Mind of Christ available to us, all his counsel, wisdom, knowledge, and understanding is open to us. We only have to ask God in faith, and he will answer.

> If any of you lack wisdom, let him ask of God, that giveth to all men liberally, and upbraideth not; and it shall be given him. But let him ask in faith, nothing wavering. For he that wavereth is like a wave of the sea driven with the wind and tossed. For let not that man think that he shall receive any thing of the Lord. (James 1:5–7)

> But God hath revealed them unto us by his Spirit: for the Spirit searcheth all things, yea, the deep things of God. (1 Corinthians 2:10)

> For who hath known the mind of the Lord, that he may instruct him? but we have the mind of Christ. (1 Corinthians 2:16)

Anoint(ing). The Holy Spirit will anoint and teach you in all truth. He will glorify Christ and illuminate the truth of God's Word, giving revelation and understanding. His anointing will abide with you and empower you to live and minister the Christian life successfully. Character and integrity is key. If you truly are a Christian, you have the ability to crucify the fleshly desires of your old carnal nature and put on Christ in the newness of God's character and grace that he gives you at salvation. We are to exhibit and produce fruit in our lives as the Holy Spirit anoints and empowers us (Galatians 5:22–25).

The anointing of God not only helps teach you and lead you, but empowers you to be witnesses to others. Evangelists are not the only ones who can lead others to Christ. The Holy Spirit will also empower you to be a witness to God's goodness and mercy to save other. Why would you wait for an evangelist to lead a loved one to Christ when you can pray for them yourselves. If they, your loved ones, will not receive the Gospel and salvation from you, don't give up, but continue to pray for them. It may be a timing issue that they are not ready to receive Christ just yet. It may be that if they won't hear it from you, that perhaps God will raise another to speak to them in a way that they can understand and receive. Whatever the case, don't give up on them. Keep praying and trust God for their salvation.

> But the anointing which ye have received of him abideth in you, and ye need not that any man teach you: but as the same anointing teacheth you of all things, and is truth, and is no lie, and even as it hath taught you, ye shall abide in him. (1 John 2:27)

> But ye shall receive power, after that the Holy Ghost is come upon you: and ye shall be witnesses unto me both in

> Jerusalem, and in all Judaea, and in
> Samaria, and unto the uttermost part of
> the earth. (Acts 1:8)

The anointing of the Holy Spirit will also give you strength to minister effectively using the gifts of the Spirit for ministry. There is a big difference of one in their own strength trying to preach, teach, or minister to someone in their own strength and knowledge. In their own strength, there may be some fruit or effectiveness; but when a person is anointed by the Spirit of God to do a work, God's super comes upon your natural ability to do the same things under his unction and power to produce a greater result because it is no longer you, but God, who is working through and with you to accomplish the task at hand.

> Then he answered and spake unto me,
> saying, This is the word of the LORD
> unto Zerubbabel, saying, Not by might,
> nor by power, but by my spirit, saith the
> LORD of hosts. (Zechariah 4:6)

Basically, God was saying to Zerubbabel that the work will be done, not by your strength/resources, nor by your power/ability, but by His Spirit of power and strength. It is this same Spirit of God and his anointing that empowers us to do the work of the kingdom.

Bring to your remembrance the Word of God. Once you read, heard, memorized, or studied the Word of God, the Holy Spirit will bring those things to your remembrance as you have need of them. But if you never put the Word in, you will have nothing for the Holy Spirit to remind you of.

That is why it is important to read, study, memorize, or even hear the Word through preaching.

> But the Comforter, which is the Holy Ghost, whom the Father will send in my name, he shall teach you all things, and bring all things to your remembrance, whatsoever I have said unto you. (John 14:26)

Glorify and testify of the Christ Jesus. The Holy Spirit is the one who will testify of Jesus the Christ/Messiah. He is the one who will bring revelation of who Jesus is. He is the one who will glorify Jesus and help us to understand Jesus's lordship, saving work on the cross, doctrine about the Christ/Messiah, and who Jesus is to us and the whole world.

> But when the Comforter is come, whom I will send unto you from the Father, even the Spirit of truth, which proceedeth from the Father, he shall testify of me. (John 15:26)

> Howbeit when he, the Spirit of truth, is come, he will guide you into all truth: for he shall not speak of himself; but whatsoever he shall hear, that shall he speak: and he will shew you things to come. *He shall glorify me*: for he shall receive of mine, and shall shew it unto you. (John 16:13–14; emphasis added)

References

Online. January 18, 2008. "Topics: Faith." *Answers by Billy Graham*. (Billy Graham Evangelistic Association).

About the Author

Pamela Delph is an apostolic prophet with a strong teaching gift. Pam is currently the overseer of World Outreach Ministries International, Inc. and Global Intercessory Prayer Network (GIN).

Pamela has helped pioneer many churches and ministries, laying strong biblical foundations, forming intercessory prayer teams and local leadership boards to govern these ministries. She has traveled overseas and throughout the United States as a prophetic speaker, minister, and is used by God in healings and miracles.

Pam is an ordained minister, author, wife, mother, and grandmother. She is currently living in the northwest suburbs of Chicago with her husband, Rick.

To contact us:

World Outreach Ministries International, Inc.
P.O. Box 3493
Barrington, IL 60011-3493

CPSIA information can be obtained
at www.ICGtesting.com
Printed in the USA
LVHW032303181220
674517LV00005B/568